A
LITTLE GIRL
NAMED
Candis

A LITTLE GIRL NAMED

A WOMAN WHO WEARS MANY HATS

CANDIS DOVER

iUniverse®

A LITTLE GIRL NAMED CANDIS
A WOMAN WHO WEARS MANY HATS

THE HOLY BIBLE, NEW INTERNATIONAL VERSION®, NIV® Copyright © 1973, 1978, 1984, 2011 by Biblica, Inc.® Used by permission. All rights reserved worldwide.

iUniverse books may be ordered through booksellers or by contacting:

iUniverse
1663 Liberty Drive
Bloomington, IN 47403
www.iuniverse.com
1-800-Authors (1-800-288-4677)

Because of the dynamic nature of the Internet, any web addresses or links contained in this book may have changed since publication and may no longer be valid. The views expressed in this work are solely those of the author and do not necessarily reflect the views of the publisher, and the publisher hereby disclaims any responsibility for them.

Any people depicted in stock imagery provided by Thinkstock are models, and such images are being used for illustrative purposes only. Certain stock imagery © Thinkstock.

ISBN: 978-1-5320-1684-4 (sc)
ISBN: 978-1-5320-1685-1 (e)

Library of Congress Control Number: 2017901720

Print information available on the last page.

iUniverse rev. date: 10/17/2017

DEDICATION

This book of poetry is dedicated to my beloved parents, Candies and Oliver Dover (Louise and Buddy), for always being there to support and love me, for teaching me old-fashioned values and how to survive. They believed in my capabilities before I did and spent their lives loving me while guiding my life with a firm hand—all the while cheering me on from the sidelines and now from heaven.

I love you, Mama and Daddy. You are the poetry and the song that lives and breathes in my heart forever.

CONTENTS

ACKNOWLEDGMENTS

I would like to take this opportunity to acknowledge and thank some very important people in my life.

To my children, André Oliver, Bronson Lee, and Richard Lewis, my three princes. The three of you are what compelled me to continue to try, the reason I never gave up! My babies have always believed in me. They loved me when I was not deserving of their love. For that I am truly grateful. Mama's biggest fans, I love you.

James and Patricia Pattenaude, who have always supported, chastened, or encouraged whenever I needed them, for opening their home and their hearts up to me, for not believing the hype. Thank you for always being positive influences in my life.

My cousin Kimberly L. Shropshire, thank you for always supporting me and for giving me sound advice. I love you!

My sister, Pamela Ann, the love that we share will never fade or dissipate. From the womb to the tomb, baby, I guess you're stuck with me!

To pastors James and Denise Love and the Real Life Christian International Church of Romulus, Michigan, thank for believing in me and my capabilities and for stirring up the gift! I love you always.

To my pastor, A. P. Barker of Faith Tabernacle World Ministries of Seattle, Washington, thank you and the Faith Tabernacle family for being there for me in many ways since my move to Seattle. Your generosity is immeasurable, as is your faith! God bless you.

PREFACE

Travel with me on a poetic journey, one that began in childhood with a gift given to everyone who is born into this world, in every man, woman, boy, and girl. That is when I discovered my voice through poetry. Follow my journey as I experience life's ups and downs. I thank God that His eye is on the sparrow, for the road to redemption for some is quite narrow. He still finds the time to watch over me. Crying without tears, trembling without fears, bleeding without injury, laughing without a smile, loving but not emotional, while becoming involved in the hustle and game of life. Faking actions and aspects of living, just getting by, living to get high, but never experiencing what life has to offer. No, it's not fiction, but a journey of escape, rejuvenation, backlash, war, and battle scars. I'm exhausted of painting a wholesome picture pretending that everything is all right, screaming out in my darkness, tossing and turning in the night. I'm changing my lifestyle, and it doesn't feel right. Change can be difficult.

A life-changing event turned my world upside-down, relapse, time-out, and not applicable came just in time. I worked some steps and got a sponsor so that I could be free. Cleaning house helps one to identify friends and foes, renewing the mind and seeking God for my soul. How foolish was I to allow myself to endure the affliction of pain and disrespect? I had to prune the tree, trim the bushes, and edge the lawn, so to speak.

Now my joy's been restored and faith renewed, running for my life, but then more bad news. Now my suffering was prolonged—please don't be mistaken. I spoke in the spirit to confuse the enemy. My soul had clearly been taken. Victory came as I embraced the knowledge of who I am. I am woman, fearfully and wonderfully made. That's who I am. Stay tuned in to this author. I certainly have more. We are women; hear us roar!

A Gift from God

↟ ↟ ↟

There is a gift given to everyone who is born into this world,
in every man, woman, boy, and girl.
God placed them there knowing that each of our lives would blossom in
due season,
that every one of us was created for a divine reason.
So if your gift has not blossomed just yet,
don't worry, complain, lose any sleep, or fret.
When others are showing off their gifts, acting as if they have it all together,
take heed and remember they don't know any better.
They are just showing off—don't believe the façade.
When *your* turn comes, please promise me that you won't forget that each
one of your gifts are from God.

A Little Girl Named Candis

🕇 🕇 🕇

I'm reaching out to a little girl in the distance, telling her to come to me
to finally let go,
to release all of those fears
so that her mind and her heart can be made free,
to stop running, stuffing, to come out of hiding, that it's okay to cry.
It's time to remove the dead weight from her spirit
so she may be free to fly.
Yesterday is her history, tomorrow's her mystery, and the present is her gift.
Don't ever allow your burdens to make you so downtrodden that your spirit
becomes impossible to lift.
Sweetheart, I know that you don't *really* believe that God has forgiven you,
but you're saved by his grace, and you're covered by His blood.
His promises remain true.
No one has ever believed or listened to you.
All of your trust was gone,
so I have gotten help and come back for you as promised. Together we can
be strong.
I'm talking to her.
I'm comforting her.
Her innocent, tiny, little world was oh-so torn apart.
I came back to let her know that she has been through too much to simply
die from a broken heart.
You see, family, it's not as if she planned this when she was that naive little girl
or even dreamed a dream of *this* capacity in her chaotic and battered
little world.

I came back as promised to let her know that she *was* a victim of circumstance but no one deliberately planned this.

If you're wondering whom I'm talking to and trying to save, the little girl's name is Candis.

Love everyone and forgive everyone,
including yourself.
Forgive your anger,
Your guilt. Your shame. Your sadness.
Embrace and open up your love, your joy,
Your truth, and especially your heart.

—*Jim Henson*

Try Being Yourself

Would my secrets be leaked if I were to speak?
They don't like me. They seldom invite me.
Am I much too ugly to matter?
Being invisible for all of my life,
Too boring to notice,
Too whorish to wife.
Why can't they see me?
I'll shorten my skirts, even change my hair.
Try unbuttoning my blouse—maybe then they would care.
A bird left in the nest never beautiful enough to fly.
I wanted desperately to fit in,
So I chose to get high.
Dope clipped my wings.
It really made me do some things.
The kind of destruction only the enemy brings.

Author's Note:
Don't ever try to be like anyone else. Stay true to yourself. The tenderness of your heart caused Christ Jesus to set you apart. Remind yourself that it is okay to fall. It is not okay to stay there. Forgive yourself.

Candis Dover

When Life Imitates Art

⚓ ⚓ ⚓

Imported tables are set with the finest china.

Scents of precious and exotic flowers fill the air.

Reflections of wine glasses are in the artist's glasses,

very similar to a quaint perfection.

In the room there is an icy chill that rises above the fine crystal glasses.

Life has given birth to the art that constantly creeps into our experiences.

Testimony of the artist patiently awaits the hearts of mankind.

We are blessed with sensations of taste, smell, sight, sound, and touch.

We are granted the ability to survive, to appreciate any element of nature

according to the *grace* of the potter who provides and navigates the clay.

Universal sensations of all God's creation are in unison.

When the most complicated of things appears to be so very simple

is when life imitates art.

Battlefield

I come from a battlefield of hurt
with landmines filled with malice,
sprinkled with shame and confusion.
Just a taste of fornication, envy, and spite are here and there
with moments of forgiveness throughout.
Without the obstacles and stumbling blocks of mercy I would still be struggling,
fighting many giants and demonic spirits alone,
bloody, broken, and ashamed.
I thank God that His eye is on the sparrow,
for the road to redemption for some is quite narrow.
He still finds the time to watch over me.
I fought for many years
through *all* of my struggles,
through some of my fears.
My Jesus wiped away every tear.
His arms were outstretched.
He held me near.
To have such a faithful friend,
to be happy once again
after all of the filthy places I've been?
What an *awesome* God we serve!
I held up the white flag.
I packed all of my faith.
I packed some of my bags
and surrendered my will to thee.

Those of us who are not familiar with such a faithful friend may never be able to comprehend what He is or who He has been.

Leave that battlefield—you don't have to go through it.

Stand firmly on the word of the master.

Praise your way through it!

He is waiting for you with arms opened wide so He can prove it.

Leave that battlefield, and run to His love.

Love Is

♦ ♦ ♦

If we allow our love to naturally flow,
believe me when I tell you the masks have to go!
I want you to see my spirit.
I would like to observe your inner glow.
Don't feel the need to save me.
I'm not looking for a superman.
Just embrace me with all of your heart.
I promise to love you as best I can.
I need you, baby, so please don't be afraid.
I vow to uphold every commitment I've ever made.
Your love is like the clouds in the bluest sky on a warm summer's day.
Baby, please won't you stay?
I couldn't survive it if you went away.
Our love is peaceful.
Our love is transforming.
Our love is magnetic.
Our love is so patient we never fight.
Baby, I want you to hold me all night.
I trust our love.
I also trust you.

Candis Dover

Your Love

Your love thrills me.
Your love heals me.
Your love nourishes me.
Your love flourishes me.
Your love needs me.
Your love feeds me.
Your love feels me.
Your love is so real to me.
Your love gives chills to me.
Your love kneels to me.
Ooh wee, the sexiness of your smile!
You rub my back with such care.
Oh, baby, I love the smell of your hair!
Your love has a panty-dropping stare.
I melt from the cologne that you wear.
I catch you watching me sleep.
Never have I felt tenderness so deep,
so sweet.
My love is all for you.

A Slave's Wedding Dress

⚓ ⚓ ⚓

My granny's wedding dress fits me just fine.

Not an old-mammy pattern—my granny was much more refined.

I finally said yes!

What a wonderful day this will be.

Marrying the grandson of our slave master so that we can be free!

Wearing Grandmother's garment is important to me.

She married my papa under that same old maple tree.

On the eve of my wedding Granny came into my quarters while the slaves were dressing me, and she said, "Oh, Candis my dear, you look so fine!"

Thank you, Granny I chose this gown from a *special* book of patterns. It's *your* custom design.

So happy I will be, and happy I will stay.

Our traditions will carry on from my very special day!

I'll tenderly kiss his forehead, Granny, after you're gone. Don't you fear.

And slit his throat with a straight razor just as you taught me, Granny, from his mouth to his ear

Meet me at the railroad about a quarter past three.

You were smart planning this before I was born. Your imagination has set us free!

Without leaps of imagination or dreaming we lose the
excitement of possibilities.
Dreaming after all is a form of planning.
—Gloria Steinem

I Can't Find My Tenderness

⚓ ⚓ ⚓

I can't seem to find my tenderness. I've searched all over—
In the closets, underneath beds, and in the garage.
Maybe I lost it when I went shopping for him.
That can't be—he screamed at me that day for losing the keys to handcuffs
that he used to imprison me.
Maybe it was the day that he pushed me down and my tooth got knocked out.
Um, I wonder.
Oh yeah, maybe it was the day I cut my hand while attempting to change
my own tire.
Or on the day dinner wasn't ready on time and he beat me with the heel
of my boot.
Someone, please stop that man!
Help me please!
The man I loved has stolen my tenderness.
Or did I give it to him?
From now on I'll place a sign on my door that reads
Do Not Enter!
Gone Fishing.
Out to Lunch.
Proceed with Caution!
One final sign will say
"I am worthy of all things that are good."

A No-Good-Ass Man

There she sits gazing off into space,
a road map of wrinkles uniquely carved onto her godly face.
Quietly she's sitting, trying to figure out if she has done everything she can
to have a piece of a no-good-ass man.
She's only left with glimpses of what her life could have been
if she had been truly loved back then.
She hardly complained,
holding those emotions captive so deeply within
just to have a piece of a no-good-ass man.
A shell of a woman is what we *now* see,
knowing for ourselves what a queen she could be.
A loving hug or a warm smile could have set this butterfly free
from a no-good-ass man.
Ladies, leave that hustler at the liquor store.
If you knew what I know, you wouldn't mess with him anymore.
Don't get caught up with his baby's mamas
or allow him to treat you like a whore.
Never throw your life away on a no-good-ass man.
At the first inkling of violence cut that evil off at the root.
If he has no relationship with God, please give him the boot!
It's past due for women to take a stand.
We must unite our voices.
We must implement a plan.
Make a promise to the warrior in your mirror.
Tell her that you will do everything you can
to never be intimidated by a no-good-ass man!

Candis Dover

Sidechick

🔒 🔒 🔒

I felt that something wasn't quite right,
so I peeked into his wallet late last night.
I saw pictures of his family,
a love and happiness that we could never share.
I had been masking my emotions as if I didn't care,
telling myself that you loved *me* more,
but your overnight bag stays packed and ready by my front door.
Nights of heated passion that we sometimes share,
then hiding in the bathroom making your phone calls there.
What we have is just an illusion,
a very deep lust.
It cannot be real.
The absence of your tenderness has created a void in my heart that only
God can fill.
From the very beginning I knew the deal.
I just needed so much to believe I could change how you feel,
trying to convince me that you're going to leave, but the timing's never right.
Whenever I ask, you want to start a false fight.
Holidays are simply the worst time of all.
I don't even get as much as a forty-second phone call
Holidays can do as much damage to my heart as you could with a knife,
yet you allow me to spend them alone
while you spend them with your wife.

> *The reason why God allowed him to walk away*
> *is because you prayed for a good man,*
> *and he wasn't.*
> —*Spiritual Word*

I Would Give Anything

I would give anything to take back that awful night.

I would give anything to make things right.

What made that woman believe that she could drive after having a few drinks?

I would give anything to be able to turn back the hands of time

so that maybe she would think!

I would give anything not to be in so much pain.

I would give anything to live a normal life once again.

I would give anything to have my career back,

for my thoughts, body, and emotional stability to be left intact.

I would give anything to not take a pill,

for pain to become unfamiliar,

but the pain is quite real.

I would give anything not to feel this way.

Doctors are clueless as to how I'm making it day after day after day.

I would give anything to feel my mother's touch.

When she was around things were better.

They didn't seem to bother me as much.

I would give anything to have a new spine.

Mine is deteriorating even though I appear to be fine.

I hear people complaining about their lives, their jobs—I find it quite odd.

If it were me, I would be dancing, shouting, praising my God!

Whenever you're late for work,

just tired,

or the alarm clock rings,

think of me and remember

she would give anything!

Baby Stripper

👠 👠 👠

Trying hard to focus, but my pocket's aren't right.
The holiday got here fast, and my money is tight.
There's a nervous feeling in the pit of my stomach I cannot seem to shake.
I know it's there because I'm in a strip club, wall-to-wall with snakes.
It's been a long time since I had to be nude and shake my bare behind.
I'll just go onto the stage, give the customers a wink, then smile.
Never let them see you cry.
Create the perfect moment for them to notice your style.
I'm telling you that deep down it really doesn't matter what you feel.
Customers don't concern themselves with the fact. Your feelings are quite real.
Just slam down a cognac. Wipe off your tears.
Allow your alter ego to rid you of your fears.
Tell the pervert at the turntable to play something slow and to make the bass pound!
Snakes are not as intrusive sliding on that stripper pole upside down.

A woman is like a tea bag,
you can't tell how strong she is until you put her in hot
water.

—Eleanor Roosevelt

Will I Wait for You?

Will I wait for you?
Not if life won't wait for me.
Tying me down to a sorry promise?
Asking if I'm free.
Listen when I ask you to let it be.
You don't miss or want *me*.
The way that I walk and the way my hips twist.
This is not a compliment; it's more of a diss.
Boy, stay off of my phone.
Please leave me alone.
I've been trying to tell you that I'm full-grown.
I can tell that your heart's just roaming without a home.
You only want to make me moan.
Your name's not Scarface.
You should feel out of place.
Please stop invading my personal space.
I'm done with your sorry self is what you need to face!

When people treat you like they don't care, believe them.
—*Maya Angelou*

Maybe Next Time

I feel a strong desire to set myself free.
Conversations and whispers on the sidelines tend to distract me.
They run at me.
It's oh so complicated and tragic!
You haven't as of yet indulged in my heart.
This body isn't all I've got.
My compassion for *others* is what makes me hot!
I'm not trying to fit in.
I don't have to get in.
Am I just a good friend?
Or nothing at all?
Would you rather I crawl?
I'm going to kiss you
then dismiss you.
I'm *sure* it's already been done.

Off-Duty

⚑ ⚑ ⚑

The off-duty sign is shining brightly on *this* taxi.
No more lying.
No more swindling.
No more being unappreciative of things I do for you.
My brakes are scrubbing.
My tires are rubbing,
but you spend all of your money *clubbing*?
Where is my gasoline?
I just may have to spank you.
Never ever exit my car with only a thank you.
You pay a taxi.
You pay a bus.
When it comes to *my* payment, you're making a fuss?
Where is my gas?
If my car stops, then we will both be walking.
Hush up with all of that mess you have been talking.
All up on my gas needle.
Why are you stalking?
I want my gas!
The next time you need a ride do not bother me.
That is wear and tear on my car that you don't see
Don't underestimate me.
Please do not assume that I'll never ask
for you to march up to that cashier and pay for my gas!

It isn't the mountains ahead that wear you down,
It's the pebble in your shoe.
—Muhammad Ali

The Mighty Oak

There's a beautiful tree in the meadow that caught my eye.
It really made my day.
What a show-off!
is what the other trees say.
But I say, *sway, tree, sway!*
The leaves changes colors in the slowest of motion.
It is really something to see.
So I sat under that mighty oak tree,
and the oak let me be.

Like a tree you have to find your roots and then you can
bend in the wind.

—Angela Farmer

God's Reign

I feel much closer to my King when it rains.
Walking in the cool breeze,
The precious morning dew all over the trees,
Who could create beauty in a manner such as this?
God nurtures the grass and the flowers
So the harvest will be plentiful for a greater tomorrow.
What a loving God we serve!
Everything has a purpose.
Everything has a season.
I tend to mess things up when my life is going well.
I *never* have a good reason.
My flesh rises up sometimes.
I tend to behave like I have lost my mind.
Things that I am most grateful for are short-lived.
I become ungrateful,
Unwilling to give.
A symbolic rainbow comes after the rain.
It seems to wash away yesterday's pain.
Whenever God sends the rainbow after the cleansing rain
He promises to never turn away from us again.
An illuminating rainbow is in front of our eyes.
We are forgiven.
You need not ask why.
In spite of all the mischief we have dabbled in,
He gave us a pass because we were *born* into sin.

My storm gave me my story.
—Detrick Haddon

Candis Dover

The Throne of God

Last night I went to the throne of God.
A majestic splendor filled the air.
Angels were singing. Lions were playing with the lamb.
Christ Jesus was loving on us from above.
Souls were being saved, crying out praises to our Savior!
God's army in full armor was preparing for battle.
I sat at my Father's feet witnessing events that brought me to tears.
I saw murder and rape,
Love and hate.
The body of Christ was judging.
Teaching of the Scriptures was minimal. There was no Christian hugging.
Fornication, sodomy,
Molestation, and armed robbery,
Bullying and strife,
Coveting your brother's wife.
My God!
Hypocrites throughout the church.
Lost, alone, and confused.
Everyone was doing dirt!
From the pulpit to the choir stands,
God was so disappointed in man.
I saw a tear fall from our Father's eye.
It made things worse to see *Him* cry.
It seems as if time is passing us by.
Believe me when I tell you God is always on time!
Give someone a helping hand.
Make an honest attempt at reclaiming our land,
Praying for one another,

Loving your sisters,

Supporting your brothers,

Being kinder to your mother,

You *do* realize that our time is drawing near?

Where would we run?

Why would we fear?

Where can we hide?

Where will we go?

Very soon we will just have to show.

When the enemy comes knocking at *our* door,

We *do not* have to accept the mark of the beast.

> *Darkness cannot drive out darkness, only light can do that.*
> *Hate cannot drive out hate, only love can do that.*
> —*Martin Luther King Jr.*

He Isn't Finished with Me

⚓ ⚓ ⚓

I shed a tear last night in prayer before I went to sleep.
I had cursed out someone I loved.
My bitterness *really* runs deep.
God took the time to design me.
He is a major part of my heart.
I communicate with Him daily,
His own *personal* work of art.
I had drawn far away from God's love because I was mad.
I felt as if I was stripped of my mom and my dad.
I had forgotten about the process.
Pain would not allow me to see.
Never had it crossed my mind the rules of life and death also apply to me.
I wasn't speaking to God.
I tried to block Him out.
I wasn't praying, wasn't worshipping,
not a murmur,
not a shout.
I started to push loved ones away
They knocked at my door.
I had nothing to say.
I did not wish to encourage.
I did not want them to stay.
So I continued to give excuses
to keep their judgments at bay.

They didn't love me anyway.
There is one thing for certain—this I truly get.
I am still a work in progress.
God isn't finished with me yet.

*Never be afraid to trust an unknown future to a
known God.*

—Corrie ten Boom

Like a Toddler

⚓ ⚓ ⚓

My curiosity is often like a toddler,
forever questioning, wondering, asking myself why.
Those are the times I break down and cry.
Circumstances that motivate the abundance of tears that flow from a temporary situation
of my personal frustration.
But the Father says,
Calm down, my daughter. Don't cry.
I was selfish, misled, just downright mean.
My thought pattern and associations were *very* unclean.
I awoke in a prison.
I wished that it was a dream.
He is.
I am.
It shall be.
I repent.
I am heaven-sent.
I came into this earth riding the wings of an angel, then was placed inside my mother's womb.
I entered this world in a *segregated* hospital room.
My earthly flesh is headed for the tomb,
but never my spirit.
Can't you hear it?
The voice of God.
I'll *never* fear it.

The Comforter is speaking through us,
because of us.
We are created in His image,
never realizing that we are royalty.

I love the Lord, for He heard my voice;
He heard my cry for mercy.
Because He turned His ear to me,
I will call on Him as long as I live.
—Psalm 116:1–2 NIV

The Poet's Game
⚓ ⚓ ⚓

They may throw dirt on your name.
The spirit is already wounded.
Getting satisfaction from your battle scars is how to play their game.
You aren't even around, but you still carry the blame?
Damn shame!
They want to jack your joy,
for you to feel the regrets of your past in their present situation.
Cowards!
Pull all those empty liquor bottles from underneath your sofa.
Don't forget the ones that are under your bed.
You're only fueling the confusion,
discord being spread.
I'm still here, honey. I'm just shaking my head.
So you want to point your finger and call *me* a whore?
Try not cutting your feet on the choirboy glistening on your bathroom floor!
See, while you were monitoring my mess you neglected to clean up your own.
Undercover crackheads always got something going on!
If my ways are whorish, then God will deal with me.
Confessing and repenting makes a sinner free.
Don't forget to blow hard before you sip on this tea.
The next time someone is slandering your name
get down and dirty—play the poet's game.
The game of truth—there's no dare included.
Play it straight up with no chaser.
The game is ineffective when you play it diluted.

We all know that cockroaches run when you cut on the light.
Don't hesitate to hit below their belts.
Keep your head held high.
You better put up a fight!
Expose those monsters—don't you be afraid.
Let them know that by continuing to throw stones
true warriors are made.

Abducted

111

I awoke in a cold and damp dwelling.
My feet and hands were bound.
My eyes were covered.
I heard her voice,
As piercing to my soul as a hot knife is to butter.
It was the voice of the accuser,
Reminding and taunting me over things that I had done wrong,
Going over mistakes I had made.
I was there for years!
I wouldn't eat.
I couldn't sleep.
Moving forward was never an option.
I was oddly focused on looking backward.
The voice spoke unto me.
She asked if I had any last requests before I took my *own* life.
So I requested to see my captor.
I wanted to look at the demonic face that had imprisoned me for all of these
years.
She became silent, and what I heard shook me to the very core of my being.
She replied,
I cannot believe after all of these years you do not recognize me.
I am your past.

Sometimes we survive by forgetting.
—*Frank Ocean*

Selfish Ass

When your heart is full and your eyes are too,
When no one cares to hear what you're going through,
When you cannot satisfy fleshly desires,
Whom do you turn to?
When your life is read like an Amazon book,
When you're judged and put to shame with just one look,
When you are forced to play nice
Or let your haters off of the hook,
What do you do with those feelings?
You have no time to hear what *I'm* going through.
Is it because our conversation isn't all about you?
Do you realize that's a selfish thing to do?
Just totally selfish, boo.
What makes you think that your tragedy is worse than mine?
Will your body rot from what you're going through?
Or is it all in your mind?
Do you pray for anyone other than yourself?
Do you *ever* find the time?
I cannot believe that you are so selfish.
All you do is whine!

To Whom It Concerns

⚱ ⚱ ⚱

Last night I had the most wonderful dream.
Everything appeared to be so beautiful,
so calming,
so serene.
I felt the arms of Jesus wrapped around me.
It was only a dream.
I thought, *How could this be?*
Awoke with my Bible in hand and, oh, how it burned!
I just thought it was real.
To whom it concerned.
Mama was cooking, and Daddy was working out back.
My dogs were in the yard playing,
the garden intact.
I awoke with only a photograph and, oh, how I yearned.
Just thought I would mention it
to whom it concerns.

> *She was brave, strong, and broken all at once.*
> —Anna Funder

Heaven

⚓ ⚓ ⚓

Today I meditated then flew above to be with some people I love.
My body was here in the physical sense,
so I lay very still.
It was extremely intense.
A single tear rolled down my face.
Time stopped in its tracks.
I was no longer in this place.
Floating,
soaring,
then flying above
to spend this holiday with people I love.
I could have visited heaven all day.
It was not my time.
Heaven would not allow me to stay.
If I had a choice, I would leave the earth at night
to come out of this earthly realm
to enter into the light.
Life, love, and the loss of someone can be a difficult situation,
so I calmed my mind,
quieted my spirit,
felt past my heart, and used my imagination.

Last night I lost the world and gained the universe.
—C. Joy Bell

Candis Dover

The Butterfly

🦋 🦋 🦋

A butterfly that flies with such grace,

Emerging from midair to land on my fingertip, speaking to my heart saying,

I am with you. Do not take for granted my presence on this day.

Bringing memories filled with love and togetherness, bright and in living color!

Recalling the times that we laughed without speaking, hugged without touching,

Cried without dropping a tear.

Two souls united, connected, fiercely intertwined!

An unbreakable bond shared by two but witnessed by many.

The butterfly that graced us with its presence will hopefully return to us in due season,

Without showing us rhyme or reason,

Emerging from her cocoon to bless my fingertips once again.

Love of the Junkie

⚓ ⚓ ⚓

Listening but never hearing,
Touching but not feeling,
Eating but never digesting,
Walking but never mobile,
Reading but not comprehending.
Crying without tears,
Trembling without fears,
Bleeding without injury,
Laughing without a smile.
Loving but never emotional.
Faking actions and aspects of living,
Just getting by,
Living to get high
But never experiencing what the senses have to offer.
What a waste of life,
of emotions.
Never finishing a sentence.
Hardly completing what was never started.
Procrastination in its worse form.
Suspended in time.
Just there for no apparent reason.
This is the life.
Mannerisms and love of the junkie.

Candis Dover

Be Still

♱ ♱ ♱

I lie here so still, so quiet, so serene,
conscious of my innermost thoughts,
my most private of dreams,
attempting to recall what just happened to me. I'm still in shock!
I never felt the surgery that He performed on my heart.
Jesus stripped me.
Jesus washed me.
My flesh is at war with my spirit.
I cast my cares upon him.
He quietly stood back and delighted in my growth.
He helped me to heal,
allowed me to fall,
then He picked me up again!
All that I require I have.
For that reason alone
I can take a moment and be still.

Change Can Be Difficult

Sometimes I cringe when I think about my past.
Same story, different decade, the contentment never lasts.
I should have stayed a bookworm.
I grew up much too fast.
Change can be difficult.
Flashbacks reappear without my permission—
Mama's singing and cooking in her kitchen,
my boys playing outside.
Damn!
It's only a vision.
Change can be difficult
even though I try to give God the glory.
Falling prey to fleshly desires is a part of my story.
I'm ready to go deeper too. Please don't ignore me.
I'm about to break down for you just how change can be difficult,
alone in a city so very foreign to me,
leaving home so that I can be free,
leaving family,
leaving friends,
my birthplace,
my history.
Change can be difficult.
I'm exhausted of painting a wholesome picture, pretending that everything
is all right,
screaming out in my darkness,
tossing and turning in the night.

I'm changing my lifestyle, and it doesn't feel right.
I'm telling you that change can be difficult.
My suitcase stays packed.
Existing, never living,
makes getting used to this life harder.
Now that's a fact!
My existence as I knew it has changed.
Sometimes I want it all back.
Change can be difficult.
I stumble forward on my quest, never to return,
unsettled and uncomfortable with some things I have learned.
I want to act a fool.
Man does it burn!
Change can be difficult.
I seem happier at times when I'm looking back.
Self-control and patience get totally out of whack.
Just like Sodom and Gomorrah,
I crave looking back.
Change can be difficult.
I pour out my heart into my poetry.
When my thoughts are on canvas I can take a good look at me.
The majority of the time I don't like what I see. Change can be difficult.

Stepping onto a brand new path is difficult,
but not more difficult than remaining in a situation,
which is not nourishing to the whole woman.
—*Maya Angelou*

Eliminating the I

I've been told to eliminate the *I*
and replace it with the word *we,*
to work some steps and get a sponsor so that I can be free.
I've finally lost the desire to kill,
to ruin,
to destroy me.
Thank God for the rooms of recovery!
I stepped outside that destructive behavior,
found a higher power whom I now call my Savior.
It wasn't easy for a person like me to get up from a life-threatening fall,
to admit that I was wrong,
to surrender it all,
to practice patience,
to gain acceptance,
to leave the streets.
Only by humbling myself could I accept complete defeat.
It was time for my heart to dance to a spiritual beat!
I'm so grateful that I'm finally free.
Look at me.
Just look at me!
If I ever get cocky or think I've arrived,
I'll just play the whole tape and remember my last high,
how I fell to my knees,
how I pleaded,
how I cried!
It's only a military attack.
The devil is a lie!

Candis Dover

Every addiction arises from an unconscious
refusal to face and move through your own pain.
Every addiction starts with pain and ends with pain.
Whatever the substance you are addicted to
—alcohol, food, legal or illegal drugs, or a person—
you are using something or somebody to cover up your
pain.

—Eckhart Tolle

Please Don't Offer Me Alcohol

⚱ ⚱ ⚱

Please don't offer me alcohol.
Coffee will do just fine.
You may want it in your system,
but I don't want it in mine.
Blackouts,
cursing out,
just out of my rabbit-ass mind!
Please don't offer me alcohol.
It's a drug to me.
Even though our state says that its legal,
I believe that I've been set free.
No more praying to the porcelain bowls
or laying on the bathroom floor because of the cold.
Please don't offer me alcohol.
I have an allergy to drugs.
If you really want to do something nice for me,
simply offer me a hug.
Double vision,
jails,
institutions, and death.
I've given away my sobriety at times.
I do not have another relapse left!
So *please* don't offer me alcohol!

I Live to Impress You?

⚓ ⚓ ⚓

Didn't you know that I live to impress you?
From my style of dress
to the heart in my chest,
I've always wondered if you knew that my swag was better than the rest.
But I live to impress you?
Is it the way I wear my hair?
Are you attracted to me?
Is that the reason you stare?
All the while pretending not to care.
Having the nerve to inquire as to what brand of padded bras that I wear?
Right down to the flower that I put in my hair?
But I want to impress you?
We both were born into sin.
You have no heaven or hell to put me in.
Are you disappointed that I won't let you win
or allow you to come in?
But I live to impress you?
You live your life according to fashion books,
always giving others dirty looks.
Feeding off the misery of others?
Religiously stalking on Facebook?
No, thanks.
I wouldn't give you a second look.
But I live to impress you?
Trust and believe I know where my blessings come from.
Certainly not from you.

Not a single one!

It's no fun when the rabbit's got the gun.

You once believed that I was trying to impress the conceded ones.

But I live to impress you?

> *People will stare make it worth their while.*
> —*Harry Winston*

Candis Dover

Giving Advice

⊥ ⊥ ⊥

Giving advice but never taking it.
Is that really how you plan on making it?
Talking about others like they'll never find out.
That's not what God is all about.
I have no room to judge you.
I know what I see.
You're rude, never humble.
Don't you even want to be free?
You never have any problems.
You never have a care,
but you want to lead people to Christ without ever having been there?
Try and be relatable.
It isn't a crime to have flaws.
For once in your life try putting away the claws.
Never making an effort to get along—
it's wrong if you don't try.
Don't you realize that we could all be dust with a single blink of his eye?
It seems as if having a good time is all that matters to you.
I speak from personal experience when I say that can be taken from you too.
Going to a building on Sunday morning does not make you clean.
How often do you reach out to others?
Do you even know what that means?
Always so messy.
Constantly gossiping.
Making jokes about neglecting to pray.
Honey, I'm here to let you know you're going to need those prayers someday.
Here is a word of caution.
Do what you want to do.
This war that were fighting is spiritual.
The enemy knows you too.

A Gossip Magazine

⚱ ⚱ ⚱

You must own a gossip magazine,
or is it that your past is snow white,
so squeaky clean?
I listen to your conversation and say to myself, *What the heck is this?*
You're always running off at the mouth. It's someone else's business.
Where was it exactly that you got your wings?
Well, I could uncover some dirt about you.
Yeah, that's right. I know some things.
The last person I heard you talking about—you need to take it back,
or I may have to tell why the brothers in the hood laugh and call you Amtrak!
Wasn't that you in the bathroom with your best friend's dude?
Now that the shoe is on the other foot, do you think that I'm being rude?
Can't you have a conversation without trying to destroy someone else's game?
Let's say we make you the target.
See if you feel the same.
It's called being put on blast. You do it every day.
You have no conversation for anyone
if you don't have anything negative to say.
So if you find the need to gossip, find something productive to do,
because what goes around comes back around.
You're drawing negative attention, boo.
Yeah, that's right. I said it.
I'm observing your scandalous behind too!

You may shoot me with your words,
you may cut me with your eyes,
you may kill me with your hatefulness,
but still, like air, I'll rise.

—Maya Angelou

Don't Step on My Heart

Please don't step on my heart.
See, it's brand-new.
Allow me to tell you some things I've been through.
Torture and pain,
Sunshine and rain,
Love, loss, and gain.
My heart is just not the same.
Little girl lost,
Little girl found.
If you place your ear over my heart,
You could hear the ocean's sound.
Allow me to make this crystal clear.
Please take special care of my heart.
To yours hold it near.

I've learned that people will forget what you said,
people will forget what you did,
but people will never forget how you made them feel.
—Maya Angelou

Pruning

⚱ ⚱ ⚱

Stress and sadness took up so much of my life,

Being fearful of letting people go who should have already been dismissed,

Thinking that loyalty was the correct answer,

But who was asking the questions?

Turning the other cheek, saying slap this one too?

How foolish was I to allow myself to endure the affliction of pain and disrespect?

I had to prune the tree,

Trim the bushes,

Edge the lawn, so to speak.

What a relief!

What a great burden lifted from my shoulders!

Having the ability to create my own peace,

My own family.

We laugh.

We love.

We share.

We care.

We love.

We learn.

We worship.

We magnify his holy name.

That is something I rarely had,

Something I longed for.

I will never again allow myself to be dismissed like garbage

Along with the stench and shame of it all.

I am no one's garbage!

Elimination was essential to the healing of my heart,

Too much unnecessary baggage,

Too much dead weight.

Are things or people holding on to you for no good reason at all?

Life is way too short for that.

If they can't show you how to love,

Show them the door.

Allow them to leave.

I have room to learn.

I have compassion.

I create from pain.

I know how to survive.

I also know how to let go,

The grief,

The bitterness,

The strife,

Memories that hurt you.

The unfruitful love that we have for one another,

Knowing all along that my ambition far outweighed my strength.

When all I had was taken from me,

I discovered that my heavenly Father was all I ever needed.

Candis Dover

Damaged Goods
⚓ ⚓ ⚓

There is a room deep inside of us.

It's called damaged goods.

The door is made up mostly of broken hearts, and calligraphy along the frame reads,

A heart that will *never* be good!

The valves and screws are dripping blood from all the lives it's taken.

Only existing doesn't sound appealing.

Spirits become infected by the aching.

Chaotic energy is flowing through our being.

Our perception has tampered with our gift.

We are not clearly seeing.

Voices whisper,

You'll *never* make it to glory.

Feeling unworthy, often silenced by haunting memories,

no one who can relate to your story.

Practicing adultery,

inciting gossip,

fornication, humiliation, shame, so many sinful mistakes.

Lord Jesus!

How our hearts ache.

I'm not leaving religion out.

Man has left his mark on spirituality as well.

Claiming to be protesting peacefully while loudly shouting out in crowd of believers,

You are going to hell!

Where is the love for your brothers?

I'm sure that you have secrets that no one knows about.

Always making sure that one of those bones you thought was buried doesn't
come flying out of your mouth.
Confessing our sins to our Lord could immediately free us all,
for all sin is counted immeasurable.
There are none too big.
There are none too small.
To be free from the bondage, the self-hatred, the shame,
to run to his arms opened wide without anger or blame.
Start to emulate what has been done for us.
Let's rid our hearts of condemnation, of malice, of hate, of disgust.
Christ Jesus bore the stripes,
the ridicule,
the lashes,
the shame.
His love far outweighed his anger.
He voiced no condemnation
and cursed no one in blame.
He was crucified on Calvary.
He took the phrase *not good enough* and nailed it to a tree,
then shed His own blood so we could be free!
Let us live our lives on purpose as Jesus Christ suggests that we should,
starting out with repenting,
while we rest assured that we are *nobody's* damaged goods!

> *The Christian does not think God will love us*
> *because we are good.*
> *But that God will make us good because He loves us.*
> —C.S. Lewis

Lashing Out

🕯 🕯 🕯

Renewing my mind time and time again,
Overshadowing mistakes haunt me,
Follow me,
Taunt me.
In the shadows, clouding my happiness,
Mistakes caused pain, misery, and regret.
Influenced by poor decisions and loneliness,
Unexpected outcomes made me angry, so I made the decision to hurt back.
Unforgivably critical of myself caused bitterness,
Then I became bitter.
My loving heart was altered,
Causing grief, despair, agony, frustration,
Yearning to be free from the guilt,
To be free from the pain,
To be free from self.
Aligning myself with a journey that has been prepared just for me.
To be cleansed,
Washed,
Free from the burden of worry
To explore gifts that were so freely given to me,
Expressing one's self in love and poetry.
I forgive the problem, chaos, lack of trust, vanity,
And I forgive me.

The natural flights of the human mind are not from
pleasure to pleasure,
but from hope to hope.

—Samuel Johnson

To Finally Be Free

⚱ ⚱ ⚱

A revolving door of boosting and tricks,
I have to get my dope or else I'll be sick.
I wish that I had never tried the damn china white.
Looks like my dealer will be getting his freak on tonight.
In the beginning using was fun. Now it's beginning to stick.
I usually bounce back.
I have to think of something quick.
I'll check myself into rehab.
How bad could it be?
To eat, get some rest,
To have an opportunity to work on me.
I will have to choose
If I want to be free.
If I still choose to use, then a casket could be my destiny.
I look all used up.
Getting sober is the key,
So I'm making a decision to finally be free.

Good Riddance

Leaving My Addiction
I gave you a part of my heart. You never gave it back.
Very judgmental and critical,
Telling lies, never giving the facts,
Giving me the confidence I thought was needed, then suddenly taking it back.
I was a slave to the orgasms that you provided,
Dying in the absence of your touch,
Crying because I depended on you so much.
My darling I loved you more.
I thought you were my trusted friend,
More dear to me than my men, my closest kin.
You turned so quickly on me!
I felt cheated, ultimately defeated,
Sick, and alone.
I was suddenly totally left on my own.
When did you stop feeling so good to me?
I traded everything for your love—
My relationships, possessions, morals, also my self-respect.
I never could keep your ass in check.
You will never use me again.
Good-bye and good riddance to my addiction!

Lost and Found

⚓ ⚓ ⚓

Lost in my twenties,
So very broken in my thirties,
From familiar hazes,
Complicated mazes, and catchy phrases.
Going around and around missing the Gospel,
Battered unfamiliar faces looking for love in all the wrong places.
Help me to testify, somebody!
I speak all day long about all that is wrong,
But what about all that is right?
There have been no major trials or frowns since I put that needle down,
Smashed that broken, jagged stem on the ground.
It never made a sound
In the alleyways where the junkies get down.
Don't worry about what you're going through right now
Even if you think that it's unforgivable.
In actuality it's very small.
One moment spent asking for God's forgiveness pays for it all!
We get a glimpse of glory by sharing the triumph in the morals of our stories.
I'm sorry—haven't you heard?
His flesh on that tree,
The shedding of Christ Jesus's blood that day on Calvary,
A living testimony that we have been made free!

Dying for a wretched sinner like me?
We should walk in love, shouldn't we?
Blessed be!
March into your victory!

> *Knock and he'll open the door.*
> *Vanish, and he'll make you shine like the sun.*
> *Fall, and he'll raise you to the heavens*
> *become nothing, and he'll turn you into everything.*
> —*Rumi*

I Belong to Him

♰ ♰ ♰

I belong to Him. He paid a great price for me.
Been keeping myself in bondage when I'm already free.
Caught up in my emotions, being so afraid to live.
I had become a taker.
I was too selfish to give.
I've been put on this earth for a purpose-filled lesson.
It almost became too late for me to realize that I had been blessed to be a blessing.
God most certainly taught me my sinful ways are not His.
For my purpose to be fulfilled I must give away what I've lived.
People often hear me testifying about the things that Jesus has done for me,
poems about him sparing my life many times the enemy would not let me be.
I took my shame and my fears and put *everything* all in.
Sex, drugs, rock-and-roll is how my poetry begins!
I want to reach others who are just as broken as me
to let them know there is a living God who loves them,
someone who can set their hearts free!
Then that would give significant meaning to my story.
How humbling it would be to change a life while giving God the glory,
not for the accolades or the fame
but to bring recognition to His holy name!
So whenever my flesh wants to get out of hand
or my heart wants to stray to the ways of man,
I will stand tall while making an effort to remain strong.
I will never forget to whom I belong.

What you are is God's gift to you,
what you become, is your gift to God.
—Hans Urs von Balthasar

Candis Dover

Heart's a-Dancing

⚓ ⚓ ⚓

Heart's a-dancing, souls romancing.

The love that you have shown me throughout my lifetime excels far beyond my expectations!

My imaginations!

My Lord!

My King!

My God!

If I had ten thousand tongues I could not praise you enough!

God of glory.

Lord of the universe!

Your presence is electrifying my soul!

When I look into the mirror I see a reflection of our Creator.

The love that I feel for you has changed my mind.

It has rearranged my life.

Sharper than any double-edged sword!

You have performed major surgery on my heart.

Matters that uses to take precedence over my life suddenly don't matter to me anymore.

Things that never mattered to me suddenly do.

Jehovah-jireh, you love the unlovable me.

Jehovah-shalom, touch the untouchable me.

I acknowledge your presence.

I relish your marvelous splendor.

My first thought when I wake in the morning,

The last on my heart before I slumber.

With every passing thought your word remains on the tip of my tongue.

Yahweh.

Jehovah-rapha.

Alpha and the Omega
Lily of the Valley
Jehovah-shalom.
The bright morning star.
I am so blessed you awakened my sleeping heart.
You are no longer a dream to me.
You are my reality,
My forever.
With every breath that I take,
With every praise I make,
Whenever my life is at stake.
I silence my mind,
Open my heart.
I am thankfully becoming aware that you are moving enormous mountains.
You are clearing away the obstacles in my life.
God's here.

Faith moves mountains, love transforms hearts.
—*John Warren*

Candis Dover

Dance, Dance, Dance

I awoke this morning with a song in my spirit!
My flesh was up and dancing,
But my ears couldn't hear it!
Many unbelievers wouldn't understand.
They may even fear it!
Just read the Word of God
You'll recognize the Holy Spirit.
He is so worthy of all my praise, but at times I just don't do it.
I would just get high, trying to get by.
If I could only pull myself through it.
Knock and the door will be opened.
Seek and you shall find.
My heart seems to be in agreement.
I just have to wrestle with my mind.
Don't be immovable like a stick-in-the-mud.
Did you know that we were legally adopted by the shedding of his blood?
Blow the dust off of your Bible, which sits on a shelf.
Pick up that mighty weapon today, and then read it for yourself.
He saved me from myself.
Now that was quite a task.
I endured self- inflicted agony
When all I had to do was ask.
Don't leave your eternity uninsured.
Place the focus on monitoring your behavior.
An honest relationship with Christ Jesus will change your life
By making Him your personal Lord and Savior.

If I were you, I wouldn't leave my eternity to chance.
Reach out, accept, and enter into His love.
Then just dance, dance, dance!

> *Everything in the universe has a rhythm,*
> *everything dances.*
>
> —*Maya Angelou*

Mighty Woman of God

⚓ ⚓ ⚓

There is a woman who reaches out to others wherever she goes.
When she opens up her mouth the anointing simply flows.
She is beautiful, humble, and blessed with an abundance of favor.
Whenever she ministers it reaches the heart.
Every word you will savor.
She is also quick to let you know she wasn't always saved.
She allows God to speak through her.
He delivers people with love and her gift of compassion,
Her heart that she freely gave.
I am a witness of this anointing.
Jesus brought me out of that dark place. My faults I could not see.
If you're wondering how he did it, it's quite simple.
She never stopped praying for me!
She never meets a stranger.
It's as if she has known you all of her life.
A mother, pastor, sister, daughter, friend,
She's also a dedicated wife.
It's an honor to follow her ministry.
In day and age that may seem extremely rare and odd,
If anyone were to inquire about her strengths, all that I can say is she's a
mighty woman of God!

> *A woman's heart should be so hidden in God*
> *that a man has to seek HIM just to find her.*
> —*Maya Angelou*

The Love of Family

I feel the love of family, as colorful as we are.
I feel the love that's near.
I feel the love that's far.
With the loving arms of generations wrapped around me so strong,
Suddenly the burden feels lifted.
I forget what was ever wrong.
Laughter, light, history, love.
My family was sent to me by heaven above.
My sisters are women of God who have always had my back,
With a word of encouragement when I seem to get off track.
A reflection of God's love for one another is what we represent.
We are favored warriors, a family who loves the Lord,
Our history of generations definitely heaven-sent!
Traditions were handed down from my mother to me
So that my children will remain in the book of our history.
We may disagree, but in the end we band together—
Children, cousins, sisters, brothers.
Never get it twisted because we really do love and cherish one another.
From the womb to the tomb is how we roll,
The clearest reflection of our Savior's soul.

Lot's of people want to ride with you in the limo
but what you want is someone who will take the bus with
you when the limo breaks down.
—Oprah Winfrey

A Poem of Gratitude

⚓ ⚓ ⚓

As I look to the sky I often wonder why I do the things I ought not do,
Why I put my fragile heart through horrific things I would not do to you.
Reminded of the times when my flesh would not let me be,
How I had been disobedient to my Father time and time again,
But yet He still forgave me.
I lacked self-control. Discipline was nonexistent.
I was speeding through my life,
From someone's daughter to someone's mother,
From someone's girlfriend to someone's wife.
I had a husband and children I was always putting first.
Neglecting my needs, tempers began to flare, and things seemed to be getting worse.
I thank God quite often for rescuing me.
Without his grace and mercy there is no telling where I would be.
This is a poem of gratitude to my Savior, my love.
I am earthbound, but God sits on high,
Blessing me from the heavens above.
Many people know my story, and then there are those who only think that they do.
It really doesn't matter 'cause these words are for my master.
Maybe they will touch your heart too.
God stepped in, blessed me, held me ever so tight.
He reached his spirit into my darkness, and He pulled me out into the light.
Some people may count the times God has saved them.
A sinner like me surely can.
He never turned His back on me.

He never behaved like man.

He gave up the ghost and died for me. I'll always love Him so.

He sent an army of archangels to save me.

He never let me go.

> *Relying on God has to begin all over again everyday as if nothing had yet been done.*
>
> —*C. S. Lewis*

It All Belongs to You

It was when my emotions began to fade that I noticed thee.
Partying my life away, all the while believing I was free.
Mercy was abundant, as was thy grace shown to me.
Imagine our love story frozen in time, etched in a book of our history.
The tracks of my tears,
The reality of my fears,
Coming to terms that it was Jesus who held me so near,
So dear.
God's grace is here!
Your spirit leaves me wanting more.
You believed I was to die for.
Love changed me.
The Word of God rearranged me.
No other love could compare to thee.
The world had left me broken.
My testimony cannot be left unspoken,
Witnessing your promises unfold, miracles to behold.
It was love that captured my sinful soul.
It all belongs to you.

The Beautiful Struggle

The room is dim and silent, but she's not alone.
The soothing crackling in the fiery embers of a warm and toasty fireplace.
Her hardwood floors look like mirrors.
She's holding her knitting needles with both of her hands.
Systematically familiar to her.
So very comforting.
She appears to be lost in the oldest of her memories,
But she is not.
She is creating new memories.
Hardly saddened by life's gains or by its losses, past or present,
The future is in her lap.
Expectations are beaming from her eyes.
Her silver hair is strong,
The length of the rocking chair itself.
Weathered skin appears tough as leather.
Signs of hard work embrace her hands and clothe her rugged exterior.
The brightest lights of her life are the souls of her children,
Her grandchildren, and generations to come.
Their lights of their lives are individually illuminating from her regal and calm demeanor.
She is holding life's lessons in the very palm of her hands,
Releasing the struggle that she once held captive deep within.

The sands of her hourglass,
Rocking and knitting,
Gaining yet releasing,
Can't you feel it?
Gaining and releasing.

One day in retrospect, the years of struggle will strike you
as the most beautiful.

—Sigmund Freud

I'm Not Here

I wonder if they will notice that I'm not here.
I left late last night,
Full of promise,
Full of tears,
Tired of this old existence,
Of not being good enough,
Full of doubts,
Full of fears.
On the trip here I remember wondering if they even realize that I have gone.
I am so happy that I left there
To go where I feel I belong,
Gone to a place where I am needed, wanted,
Guided, and loved,
Not taken for granted or ridiculed,
Never pushed,
Never shoved.
I am not being selfish.
I don't care if you think that I'm wrong.
I'm wondering if they have even realized that I am long gone.
You don't have to call.
Don't try and look for me.
Please don't be so kind.
The only heart that skips a beat in my chest from aching is mine, all mine!
Divided we stand.

Divided we fall?

So why would you waste your time now with a silly little phone call?

The young rebel inside me says, "Woman, don't you fear."

But the inner child cries out, "Do they even notice that I'm not here?"

> *Hate is too great a burden to bear. It injures the hater*
> *more than it injures the hated.*
>
> —*Coretta Scott King*

Spreading My Wings

Is it the things that I do
Or the people that I know?
The Word of God says that we shall reap what we sow.
I was hopeless, broken, helpless, and afraid.
I took a much-needed inventory of my life and what a mess I had made.
Every so often I would gaze up at the sky
And would orchestrate an escape route each time I got high.
Unexplained to many, 'cause baby I have had given plenty!
But having an explanation?
I don't owe to any!
My heart created an echo.
I had nothing left.
The enemy had a hold on my soul,
So I created a spiritual death.
A death to the loneliness,
A death to the fears,
A death to the aching,
A death to my tears.
Now my suffering was prolonged. Please don't be mistaken.
I spoke in the spirit to confuse the enemy.
My soul had clearly been taken.
The enemy had been cast down long ago.
I can remember reading that in his word.
My spiritual senses needed to be awakened.
I was behaving as if I had never heard.

Candis Dover

I'm going to reintroduce myself back to myself, speak my mind, and spread my wings.

My mother used to always say to me, "Mama Maria, you are special. You are going to do *unbelievable* things!"

> *He reached down from Heaven and rescued me. He drew*
> *me out of deep waters.*
>
> —*Psalm 18:16*

A New Hunting

🔔 🔔 🔔

Billie Holiday blessed us with her testimony in a song called "Strange Fruit,"
Our brothers swinging from trees
When all they ever wanted from this life was to be free.
Emmett Till's battered frame is still swinging.
It's that same old negro spiritual.
Can't you hear the church bells ringing?
Protest signs should read Kumbaya or Bust!
Oh dear God, the police are killing us!
From 2003 to 2009, 4,813 of our people died.
That means 4,813 of their mothers cried.
The majority of the police got by.
Were the jurors getting high?
Just to get by?
Did they cry?
I sigh.
I ask myself why!
Michael Brown was shot to death,
Eric Garner was choked till he had nothing left.
He strained. "I can't breathe!"
Till his very last breath!
Our communities were devastated and hurt.
All we got was a T-shirt.
Trayvon Martin was only a kid.
Hey, George Zimmerman, we know what you did!
It used to be southern trees that bore strange fruit.
With blood on the leaves,
With blood at the root.

Now it's all over our great nation.
Can't you just feel the mounting frustration?
What the police needed is a permanent vacation,
Not another demonstration!.
A twenty-five-year-old mentally ill man called Ezell was shot two times
for practice.
Once in his back.
He wasn't a threat to anyone.
Can you believe that?
My spirit just cannot receive that!
Okay, I'm back,
And I'm *still* black.
How about that?
Our men no longer swing from those strange fruit trees.
Police aren't only wounding them,
Only aiming at their knees.
They're killing our babies in cold blood as proudly as you please.
They're aiming for our hearts.
Dear God, it's a slaughter.
They're trying to make us extinct
By murdering our sons,
By murdering our daughters!

Murder begins where self- defense ends.
—Georg Buchner

Many Pulses Were Silenced on This Day

Time is up to live,
To laugh,
To work,
To play.
Their time on earth has been cut down.
The victims were never given a say.
Many pulses were silenced on this day.
Please pay close attention, comrades. America is in a crisis,
Citizens walking around toting assault rifles
While pledging allegiance to Isis?
Media reports that he frequented the club, bewildered by his own sexuality.
He orchestrated and carried out a plan that demanded a homophobic killing spree.
Where is their security in this land of the free and home of the brave?
I wish their precious lives could have been saved!
Many pulses were silenced on this day.
Some of the victims hid under the dead.
Some were trying not to cry.
Some called to say I love you to a loved one,
I'm afraid,
Some for their final good-bye.
He was on the radar of the FBI,
And they still had to die?
Many pulses were silenced on this day.
This poem is dedicated to the Orlando victims.
Our country should remember their names
For living their lives out loud.
In color,

No guilt,
No regrets,
No shame.
They didn't try blending into this world all by themselves, unique.
They were daughters and sons,
Cherished by many,
So often deciding to turn the other cheek.
To thine own self be true.
If being true to yourself could cost you your own life, that must be a difficult thing to do.
To my rainbow-colored sisters and brothers,
I see you.
I see you.
We must find a way to protect our country,
The citizens who live therein.
Whenever senseless murder occurs in our nation, its the evil that lurks within.
Did you hear me?
Should I say that again?
No one should have to live in paranoia, shame, or fear.
Seek a higher calling for your own lives. Stop judging.
God's here.
It's our only hope as a nation.
It's the only sensible way.
We shouldn't lose our lives
Because of our hearts.
Many pulses were silenced on this day.

> *Bigotry murders religion, To frighten fools with her ghost.*
> —*C. C. Charles Caleb Cotton*

Edward Sotomayor Jr., 34
Stanley Almodovar III, 23
Luis Omar Ocaslo-Capo, 20
Juan Ramon Guerrero, 22

Antonio Davon Brown, 29

Akyra Monet Murray, 18

Luis Daniel Conde, 39

Eric Ivan Ortiz-Rivera, 36

Peter D. Gonzales-Cruz, 22

Eddie Jamoldroy Justice, 30

Darryl Roman Burt II, 29

Deonka Deidra Drayton

Alejandro Burrios Martinez, 21

Anthony Luis Laureano Disla, 25

Jean Carlos Mendez Perez, 35

Franky Jimmy De Jesus Velazquez, 50

Martin Benitez Torres, 33

Luis Daniel Wilson-Leon, 37

Christopher Joseph Sunfeliz, 24

Mercedez Marisol Flores, 26

Xavier Emmanuel Serrano Rosado, 35

Gilberto Ramonsilva Menendez, 25

Geraldo A. Ortiz-Jimenez, 25

Simon Adrian Carrillo Fernandez, 31

Oscar Aracena-Montero

Miguel Angel Honorato, 30

Javier Jorge-Reyes, 40

Joel Rayon Paniagua, 31

Jason Benjamin Josaphat, 19

Cory James Connell, 21

Juan Chavez-Martinez, 24

Jerald Arthur Wright, 31

Leroy Valentin Fernandez, 25

Tevin Eugene Crosby, 25

Jonathan Antonio Crosby, 25

Jean C. Nieves Rodrigue, 27

Rodolfo Ayala-Ayala, 33

Brenda Lee Marquez Mc Cool, 49

Yilmary Rodriguez Solivan, 24

Christopher Andrew Leinonen, 32
Angel Candelario-Padro, 28
Enrique L. Rios Jr., 25
Kimberly Morris, 37
Frank Hernandez, 27
Paul Terrell Henry, 41

Strength of a Woman

The strength of a woman is her heart.
She is all by herself,
Raising her family without a man around.
She doesn't have any help.
She prays that her children will one day have a chance.
She worked for all of those years just to beg the government for food stamps.
She never cries in front of the children to not appear weak.
When she's in her bedroom she cries herself to sleep.
She was judged by people in the hood on her looks, body, and hustle.
If she were lacking any of these, my dear, she had to struggle,
Praying for the safety of her children day and night.
She shelters, educates, tends to their wounds when they get into a fight.
Anyone who's never experienced this may never know
How deep a mother's love for her children can go.
She's being bullied and scrutinized. There is no husband in the home.
The dope boys from the hood are coming at her strong!
She's all alone.

Author's Note:
I am a single mother. My experiences are from where I speak. This poem was not presented in poor taste. It's my opportunity to teach. It could be my opportunity to reach. Single mothers have done something special that many people cannot do. So from the beginning, the middle, and the end of your parenting, I'll take my hat off to you!

Once you know who you are,
you don't have to worry anymore.
—*Nikki Giovanni*

A Woman, That's Who

⚓ ⚓ ⚓

For a total of nine months, in her womb she carries a life.

In between time she is a mother, cook, teacher, wife

Who is always prepared to give her husband a much-needed hand?

Or can handle some of the worst pain known to man?

A woman, that's who.

Who can chastise her own children whom she loves the most?

Who can tell bedtime stories?

Then look under beds for imaginary ghosts?

Who can sing her family to sleep with the most precious of lullabies?

Who can watch her child fall?

They laugh.

She cries?

Who can bleed for seven days and still not die?

A woman, that's who.

Watch out now, 'cause we're knocking down doors.

No one's honey, hookers, bitches, or whores.

Stay tuned in to this author.

I certainly have more.

We are women. Hear us roar!

Made in the USA
Middletown, DE
19 March 2018